10:10

Also by Michael Trussler

Poetry
Realia
The History Forest
Rare Sighting of a Guillotine on the Savannah
Accidental Animals

Non-fiction
The Sunday Book

Short Fiction
Encounters

10:10

MICHAEL TRUSSLER

icehouse poetry

Edited by Jim Johnstone.
Cover and page design by Julie Scriver.
Cover images detailed from Johannes Vermeer, *A Lady Writing*, c. 1665 (public domain); "Interior view of *The Beanery* by Edward Kienholz," CC BY-SA 3.0; Pieter Bruegel the Elder, *Hunters in the Snow*, 1565 (public domain); and Johannes Vermeer, *The Art of Painting*, c. 1666-1668 (public domain).
Printed in Canada by Rapido.
10 9 8 7 6 5 4 3 2 1

Library and Archives Canada Cataloguing in Publication

Title: 10:10 / Michael Trussler.
Other titles: Ten ten
Names: Trussler, Michael, 1960- author.
Identifiers: Canadiana 20240351363 | ISBN 9781773103389 (softcover)
Subjects: LCGFT: Poetry.
Classification: LCC PS8639.R89 A613 2024 | DDC C811/.6—dc23

Goose Lane Editions acknowledges the generous support of the Government of Canada, the Canada Council for the Arts, and the Government of New Brunswick.

Goose Lane Editions is located on the unceded territory of the Wəlastəkwiyik whose ancestors along with the Mi'kmaq and Peskotomuhkati Nations signed Peace and Friendship Treaties with the British Crown in the 1700s.

Goose Lane Editions
500 Beaverbrook Court, Suite 330
Fredericton, New Brunswick
CANADA E3B 5X4
gooselane.com

To Lloyd Trussler (1939–2022) and my family

Those who are truly contemporary, who truly belong to their time, are those who neither perfectly coincide with it nor adjust themselves to its demands.
    — Giorgio Agamben, "What Is the Contemporary?"

Contents

The Mountains Are Hallucinating

Nachträglichkeit ↔ *Nachträglichkeit*

The colour white begins

with eggshell. Surrender's
wave. Knotted
underwear, worn on

the cross. The baby teeth
your father kept for you
in a Japanese box.

2.
Because the colour white makes illness
easier; check out the fingernails
of everyone here. Because the colour white, when
careless, churns out aphorisms; check
out that Russian painter, the one
whose brush tore the drama
from monologue — its
blood blown across
the scarcest snow.

What's the hurry?

3.
I lie in a red box. A torso
for collectors only. Wax over
bisque porcelain. My hair, they
say, could be human.

What's your hurry?

Every love song is grey
flour between your fingers.

4.
Bleached, the sun's a violin.
An owl's claw. And the soul

suspends its worth. The colour white
face down on a deluged
sidewalk.
Reflected, trees initiate.
Shepherd infinitude
into dimensions
of rising cloud. White, always
beyond
        the whispered return
of stolen things / staring,
colour reeling
inside
us:

5.
an elderly Jewish woman on TV last night gave me this gift, a mitzvah
that I'm passing on to you. After surviving the camps, she found
herself destitute in what remained of Europe. She fell in love with a
man. He fell in love with her. They wanted to get married, and she felt
bad that she couldn't have a wedding like the ones she remembered
from her childhood. Her husband-to-be promised her a white wedding
dress. But how to get one? His response: with a kilo of coffee and
some cigarettes, he bought a parachute on the black market. It had
once been used by the Nazis. He dragged the parachute, a silk cloud,
across recurrent fields to a tailor, who then fashioned a virginal dress
from the material. She was married in it. And so, eventually, were
seventeen other brides.

Rectangles

The rectangle is a great human invention.
  — Brice Marden

A spider's web?

You can tell

           she's a Vermeer
from down the hallway, the light half / way
between tequila, frayed lemon, and sand.
She's writing, maybe a letter, maybe
something else: none of us on this side
of her will ever know. Within her face
a glow you've never worn, but welcome
immediately —
           The white fur
edging
the jacket that's keeping her warm
is another way of saying
she's in between
words or
sentences, that turning place
when thought's about to happen.

It's

(a little like
swimming hard and finding
a sandbar
or when a child suddenly points out
in a zoo an animal she recognizes
that until then had lived mostly as a picture
on a page in a book)

           when the precise
self becomes water / which isn't
what time is exactly, but for us, is what irreplaceable

2.
means. Eager, you become intent on sending
her a postcard, maybe even hers, the one you
just bought in the gift shop, the one
now in your hand, just to tell, just to

tell her   what?

(Not the back flash of the seconds moving
between us: nor the necessary bindings
of anyone's biography: Instead)

this: how a glacier sounds —
                    Catch a suitcase tossed
                    from the sky, once called
                    the heavens, all full of the earth's unhurried
                    heirlooms

3.
If I could parachute from here
to Delft in 1665, I would do it
instantly, and the three of us (Vermeer, you,
and me, the stranger) would jump up and down on the silk cloud
that's suddenly come from the future, something we'll decide
we have to hide. Later we get drunk down several streets
and before I find myself back here I pull both of you close.
                    Listen, I say,

I can't offer anything in return. That matters. It doesn't. Only
three hundred and eighty four people who have ever lived
have been able to make something new. All I can do is make
up all (over again) what's greater than me / somehow meet

what happens once —

4.
When a glacier breathes, Johannes, it releases ravens. When
a glacier breathes, earth grinds against the greyest sky. When
                                        Without
pain —
        morphine hiccups split
time

into a spray   of snow

Rectangles

It's mostly dark, but I can count sixteen of the most gentle arches on the ceiling. There's a damp-wood smell. Those two rectangles, made of unwhispered yellow over the red, scored floor, wouldn't have been here when this boxcar was taking people somewhere inside Poland. Those rectangles, their Rothko hum, made from the warm museum light passing through today's slatted windows in this unsoiled cattle car, are outside of what passes as *now* in the Holocaust Memorial Museum in Washington, DC, a place that's only a brief walk from Vermeer's painting of the young woman pausing over what she's writing to look up at us at some point during the seventeenth century.

The choice is yours:
you
can enter the boxcar and stand
where others
                    have been, or
you can bypass
the exhibit, leaving
what's innocent unseen —

They've never smelled jet fuel

these hunters in the snow, the trick of time,
its motion
being more than we can grasp. But we
can at least gape at colour underneath
this rizzened green that scores cuts
in a pond's ice made by skaters
and how bark feels unlike
snow in the hands.

It's amiss   that the green he made the sky hold within itself is
in only one place, stays inside a room in Vienna, where it remains
        loosely
apart from Bruegel's nearby hunters. Both nearby and vanishing
they're tired with a weariness
                                that spreads out
from the spine; they're tired and returning home in
February 1565, while the unseen sun's astray from its usual path
above an expanse of chimneys, most of them doing their proper
        work
with the exception of one ablaze not so far away, this one hinting
onough that tho drapod fox muct havo loft como blood
                                flushed somewhere
that's missing from view, its unforeseen and fading colour
eventually reminding me of a postage stamp from España I must
have glued into a childhood album a few centuries away
        from what's suddenly
happened. And now an arriving magpie's white, black,
and coiled sheen is
                        free falling and heedless, untroubled by every
fever, its calling kin to kin a madrigal like laughing   like finding

Japanese green tea picked in the springtime and within this
        bounty   two

of the men's spears meet briefly to make an isosceles triangle,
a moment's nest, a sloping
mirage of disengaging form. Our footprints, we
learn, must abandon

what keeps
happening
                to the wary
and impetuous dead

and each of
us is returned
to our place —

When You Sat for Dix
After Portrait of Dr. Heinrich Stadelmann by *Otto Dix*

You knew he'd kill.
We were made to surrender. A gift
of a kind. Nothing
             you'll ever know—

You want me to talk about Zeppelins. Yes, I saw several. I saw
other things, too. Just ask. If you know how to open
what keeps missing. My neighbour's daughter once sold
her rabbits to send money to Count Zeppelin, to replace one
of his failing
ships. That was before
the First World War, when I'd set up my first
clinic in Dresden. I saw him, once, and would have
voted for Eckener against
Hitler, but we didn't get the chance
to do
that, did we? I know what no one
can remember. All of them. Ash. My neighbour's daughter and her own
daughters fast upon that
February in 1945.
Zeppelins?
Their brochures said that flying
on the *Viktoria Luise* or the *Sachsen* would make
anxiety and doubt disappear
like streaks of mist…and if everything
is true at least once, then an airship
comes from bricks once made from
bombed houses stacked into correct piles in streets by women
the Russians didn't leave
behind in Berlin. I've written books that start by vanishing, kept
company
with the most amazing
of birds, fired
a gun into the champagne glass you

can't believe is still in your hand: believe
me, none of us is even one
of history's stowaways.

Born alongside a time of imbecility, someone might earn a doctorate,
a licence, and then lose all savings in Dresden one morning in 1922,
receive ersatz honey in lieu of a fee during the next war. Practice
psychiatry instead of Aristotle's 2/3. Be sympathetic to Dada, and
love one M. von H. until no one could do anything beyond hypnosis
and the necessary séance. Equal to these nearby thugs and Bach
who keeps staggering an owl's maybe. A wooden rhino might once
have been nailed onto a piece of actual Corinth amidst flowers that
will never be invented:

because my spirit hurts so with arthritis: dull teeth witnessed from
beneath the skin.

The Temptations of Saint Anthony

Two skeletons share one tongue: a kinship
passed through moral

necrophilia and a cavalcade of simple
fabrications   her dress never   the less glimmering
with the perpetual temptations of Saint Anthony —

One of her arms ends in a prosthetic guitar and the other's
a candle for cleaning the cuts she makes when she's
soaking in the bathtub   she's impossible to please
when she steps naked amongst us   she's the indigo flicker
between what's visceral   and what's faraway
what's inventive   yet true to life   we are accidental
scaffolds of immediacy built around the floating infinite

(its astonished playground by the derelict seaside where
        the essential shipwrecks occur

as beauty walks through us like an abandoned
disciple's dream of finally having left behind
the need for continuous prayer)

2.
And tonight I sense you here waiting   here where it's always
new again   this uprooting   this dirty and aseptic grief
that finds how

little the soul really holds   its few favourite words   its one
road its eyes here and astray   how in thousands hardly anything

except

what we have to pay back   though we're never told what
it is precisely that we owe when   we find ourselves infirm
and as deserted

as Eurydice   this needing to visit each   other once more
the sweetest trap is being   offered a second chance to slip past
what's irreparable   a longing   that guts me   this longing that

annihilates the discipline
of both the solitary and communal mind —

The sky underlit with concrete

and red Braille. Only yesterday, for instance, I forgot
how to make a paper airplane for my son.

This is a game we play:

Him: What's a tattoo?
Me: A sleeping mirror.

Him: What's a mirror?
Me: A cupboard that's quiet.

Him: What does quiet mean?
Me: It's when you feel your corn snake, Buddy Buttercup, breathing
while you hold her in your hands.

Him: What's holding something in your hands?
Me (saying, finally tired): It's when

your shopping cart is empty but you should
give it
a purpose

Click.

Someone threw newly arrived inmates into the quarry at Mauthausen
and joked that they were paratroopers. Someone else improvised a
parachute beneath a studio's skylight in Manhattan because painting
is daybreak on a shelf crowded, no, ravened with

                              tenderness
A topic for another life:

Everything After Follows from That
(An Elegiac Conversation)
For Dave Reynolds

Remember how long you have been putting off these things, and how often you received an opportunity from the gods and yet have not used it. You must now at last perceive of what kind of universe you are a part, and the true nature of the lord of the universe of which your being is a part, and how a limit of time is fixed for you, which if you do not use for clearing away the clouds from your mind, it will go and you will go, and it will never return.
— Marcus Aurelius, *Meditations* 2.4

Image from Len Carey's series *Nothing Remembers the Continuous*

The following conversation took place by email during the late summer of 2022 between the journalist and art commentator Grant Stonehouse and mixed-media artist Len Carey. Portions of the exchange have been reconstructed from the imagination.

Grant Stonehouse: How is your health?

Len Carey: They didn't used to ask questions like that one: how is your health?

GS: Everyone's getting older. I guess now's your turn.

LC: Fair enough. I now have reasons for not trusting my body like I once did. On the other hand, there's this lovely sense of virtue in consuming organic blueberries, sleepless kale, and the purest of clear tequilas. But my memory's imprecise in ways it's never been before.

GS: What do you mean?

LC: I once could trust that when I started a project that would take a couple of years, the person who finished it could unhesitatingly recall how it felt to begin the whole thing, from idea to notes to practice. Now I'm several different people, few of whom I can remember. What worries me (to be clearer, what almost deranges me with fury and fear) is: what if *everyone* my age is experiencing this deterioration but won't admit it? I mean: we're stuck on a planet run primarily by damaged people way past their sixties and what if pretty well everyone who's middle-aged (or older) is screwing up, but they're unwilling to make the appropriate adjustments?

GS: I always loved when interviewers describe the location in which the interview took place. Communicating with you over email, I can't do that. When you look around, what do you see?

LC: There's some birds fighting over the dead bugs in the radiator grill of the SUV parked way too close to this window. Sam Shepard's *Day out of Days* lying face down on the floor. A plastic Australopithecus Mommy beside the shaving mirror. It's almost dark and there's the most beautiful thing anyone can see: the word VACANCY spelled out in thin, orange letters. Neon's hue of disastrous perfection. The mountains are disappearing. I must be in a motel.

GS: So, you're on holiday.

LC: More or less, though many would say that people like me are always on holiday.

GS: If you're in a motel now, could you describe your usual workspace?

LC: I once fell in love with a Mondrian exhibit. His studio in New York must have been like the sound of a match striking. There was hardly anything there: floor, walls — almost nothing but open space. What I remember best is the wooden stool he made. It was the sort you'd stand on to water plants. Except there were no plants. He hated green. When he was on a train, he'd turn his head away from the window, just to avoid green. If you looked at the stool closely, you'd notice how many angles and rectangles he'd used. I regret that I don't think as precisely as he did. There's only one stool in the world like his. Or was. Who knows where things end up? I don't have that purity. When I work, I'll often put a movie on: recently I kept replaying *Andrei Rublev*. A brilliant movie about colour versus history and how one of them always wins. Just before I came here, I kept shuffling pictures I'd taken of Rembrandt's painting of Aristotle contemplating a bust of Homer: he looks like an aging biker who's suddenly struck it rich. There are numerous toy soldiers, some antique, quite a few of them trying to find the right target. Many aim at the door. There's something I should probably throw out, just in case it's poisoning the air: the feathers and claws I cut from a Blackburnian warbler that flew into a window just over a decade ago. What's left is in a zip-lock bag, taped against the wall. A fossil mosasaur's tooth inside a bus station–diner coffee cup I've kept from London, Ontario. I often listen to music repetitively: some Lou Reed, Tim Hecker's *Ravedeath, 1972*. Certain tracks from David Bowie's *Heathen*.

GS: Are you listening to music now?

LC: A mixture of Einstürzende Neubauten and some watered-down Mozart. When I'm thinking about Rothko, which is often, I pay attention to Morton Feldman. His music for Rothko's chapel. The lovely migration of musicians trying to learn from painters who sometimes made claims about poetry. I guess this puts the pin

through my thorax. An hour ago, Laurie Anderson's *Homeland*.
But that's a different story.

GS: What did you do today?

LC: I hiked up Ha Ling Peak. Showed me like a bitch how old I'm
getting. I almost gave up several times. Until today, I hadn't
realized how mountains reach into you. Up on the top the wind
kept everyone low; it was so fierce. There was this couple who'd
passed me on their way up, and, as we exchanged cameras on
the peak, I could sense more than a dash of schadenfreude.

GS: You were envious?

LC: Of course. I always think in terms of life's arithmetic. If they're
lucky, they'll have fifty more years of hiking, whereas I have
considerably fewer, maybe ten — fifteen, tops. That's if
everything goes to plan. But I don't envy only their youth. After
they made the hike, stood on the peak, they then lay back
against the mountain in a slight cavity, which protected them
from the wind. Held hands. Maybe closed their eyes as they
lay side by side. I've never learned how to do this. Lie down in
the open. Let a moment leave me alone. Can't be done. Nope.
And then, of course, they passed me while going down the
mountain. It was a pleasure to see them later that night on a
patio restaurant on Main Street; so, I sent them an anonymous
bottle of wine.

GS: I know this question is usually kept until the end, but what are
you working on?

LC: Why be so abrupt? Wouldn't it make sense to ask what the trail
conditions were like, what kind of wine everyone was drinking
that night? Anonymous details matter. What I'm working on just
now keeps changing, but it goes something like this: there's
a train, heading to Normandy, one of those trains that has
cabinets on one side, an unsteady hallway on the other. There
are three people sitting across from you who keep shifting
because of the hand-held camera: Ai Weiwei, Marcel Proust,

and Heinrich Himmler; and each of them notices that you're reading Peter Longerich's biography of the Reichsführer. I imagine that this book will be the last one written on Himmler. Meanwhile this old guy keeps showing up all the time: at every station he's knocking at the door: he's got to find his cat and let him outside so he can look at the seagulls. Do you know anything about that?

GS: Why have public spaces suddenly become important to you? Nothing you've done before involved park benches, or those truncated seascapes on a playing field, for instance.

LC: Your use of the word "suddenly." How wonderful. Thank you. My best friend stole the coffee cup I referred to earlier from a bus station diner. Gave it to me for Christmas. Maybe one day I'll give it back to him, *suddenly*.

GS: Your earlier work was meant to be displayed indoors. *Burning* (minus) *4* involved miniatures within refrigerators. Your recent work with park benches is subject to accidents. One was partially destroyed because of two dogs fighting. At least the video camera recorded it all.

LC: Let the benches be attacked by jackals riding werewolves, if need be. It's part of the show. Those fridges, BTW, had been placed in different places to weather first. Each for two years. And Montana is different from what Florida or Amsterdam can do. I'll let you in on a secret: when Sven Nykvist died, one of his fans took a crowbar to three phone booths in downtown Stockholm. Imagine that: a city with phone booths. Wish she'd gone after one of my fridges. I'm also working on a series that begins like this: the audience sees something of Mondrian's, and then an axe cuts through the canvas from behind. It doesn't take long. You'd be surprised at how varied the reactions are. Everything after follows from that.

GS: But why video now? Why holographs? Almost all of your work's been painting, photography, the occasional chalkboard.

LC: Beuys did chalkboards first. Whatever I did was in homage. Painting isolates what happens when you try to put things together, but there's something about incoherence that's hard to manage with static images. A master like Leon Golub can do it, but I'm not a master. You want to take on different kinds of deliberate evasion, chance, and obsession, but certain things remain problematic. These days I prefer video because video's so accurate, and also it's so spiritually crude. There's a part of me that just can't wake up in the morning, so I spend the rest of the day with a part of me saying yes, no, yes, to what consciousness not so much ignores, as misses entirely. It's like there's this stream in the back of my head that keeps falling asleep. My work is precisely the adult's attempt to restore not so much the previous innocence of childhood as its sudden and oceanic incoherence. Video embodies something of that. Have you seen any of Joseph Cornell's movies?

GS: Cornell made movies?

LC: It's mostly Cornell addicts who know about them or go to where they were made. He often spliced together bits from incommensurate films or followed pigeons around a fountain. Park benches were like Alice's looking glass to him. The man was perfect because he was both ahead of and behind his time, and likely couldn't have told the difference between them.

GS: Who are the artists you've been thinking about lately?

LC: Depends what you mean by either demarcation. Anselm Kiefer gives me more chances than I deserve, but because I don't speak German memory, I'm limited to imagining what remains the very second his hand has left the canvas or put down the blow torch. Christian Boltanski. Ori Gersht. A Caspar David Friedrich painting I don't remember ever having seen. Vermeer, always. Some time ago, the Met held a retrospective of Robert Frank's *The Americans*. Spent my time in front of his streetcar-in-New Orleans shot. Somehow, he gave breathing room in that photo to every important movement since 1904. I've been trying to do something like that these days, what Frank did: meld a distanced realism with an odd kind of political expressionism, but in an almost-forgetful-but-now-I-remember-it kind of way.

GS: I understand Vermeer and Frank, but Friedrich?

LC: Friedrich understands what it means for a moment to pass. He's utterly different from Monet, a painter who also thought about moments; but for him, it's a calibrated trembling. The colours vibrate all on their own: they're meant for the receptive human eye. Monet wants to know the instant in terms of *now*. But Friedrich looks at the second that happens *after* that original moment. His colours are diffuse, enormous, almost unfamiliar, and in their refusal to be nailed down, they have no lasting interest in how they're perceived. He understands that we have no means either of comprehending or articulating what it means to be faced with these things.

GS: Some of your recent work features someone named Dave Reynolds.

LC: There's an historian with the same name, but I don't mean him. Dave was a boy I knew when my family lived in England when I was young. We went to school together. He had a scar on his upper lip that embarrassed him terribly. Everything shrugs its shoulders. I discovered by accident that he'd killed himself after serving in the Falklands War. I've tried hard to learn what exactly happened, but no one at the other end in England will answer.

GS: I know who Jizchak Löwy is, because I saw his image flicker in the Franz Kafka Museum in Prague. Löwy keeps showing up in your recent work. Can you tell us about him?

LC: Not very much. He was one of Kafka's most carefully chosen friends. He was a Yiddish actor whom Kafka's father derided. He lived in Paris and then returned to Poland, thinking maybe about his problems. Ended up back in Warszawa. Let me email you a photograph: in it, there's a glass of wine, a box of bread across from an empty chair. I took this picture in a hotel in downtown Warszawa, after having taken a cab to the Umschlagplatz Monument — *Umschlagplatz* means the "taking-away place" — which is the last open space that Löwy would have seen before being transported to Treblinka. If he hadn't been Kafka's friend, you and I wouldn't be talking about him now. On the monument, there's a list of first names. Abigail to Zygmunt. Until I took the picture, I hadn't realized how irony becomes a meaningless constant that argues with guilt. Apart from a cluster of sentences in Kafka's diaries, the closest I would get to him was getting out of the cab that early evening and crossing the street to Umschlagplatz. Later, in the restaurant, I continued this kind of false daydreaming. I imagined him in the present, wanted him to choose something from the wine list, decide on his favourite cheese; but, as I started to pass the bread to him, the dish struck a thick, and now suddenly dirty, plastic partition between us with a smack, and he disappeared: it's more than a little self-serving, but I hallucinate often.

Last Monday I watched *A Film Unfinished*, a documentary that contains sections of a movie the Nazis made in the Warszawa Ghetto to show how disgusting they are: Jews — and here's how they should make you feel. That the images are unbearable is the smallest part of what happens. You become suspicious of every motive regarding what it means to watch this movie. You're not a victim, nor a perpetrator, nor a witness. Almost everyone in front of you is going to end up at Treblinka. A child dances with the hope for money. There it is, everything, on a street that can't ever have happened. I need to go over this movie slowly, with a magnifying glass, as it were. Perhaps if I do this often enough, I'll see Löwy. Or what Korczak might have seen.

GS: What other documentaries do you return to?

LC: Herzog once made a movie in a cave. It hasn't been disturbed for over thirty thousand years. He's there because of the cave paintings. And he discovers that a late-Paleolithic artist started a rendition of some kind of animal, let's call it a reindeer or a bear or some other creature that's extinct, and for reasons we'll never know, this artist didn't finish it … but five thousand years later, someone new came along and *completed the painting*. Gave the previous artist a kind of high-five. And then, along comes Werner. Imagine somebody in ancient Sumer writing part of a poem, and then someone else picks up those very threads last year (maybe you if you write poetry), moves from one stanza to the next and decides to finish the poem. Could you do it? Everything staggers. What within could help you try to do something like that? Such joy.

Grant Stonehouse has written widely on visual artists. He has a forthcoming article (in the journal *November*) on the semiotics of taxidermy in the work of assemblage and installation artists such as Edward Kienholz.

Len Carey works in photography and mixed media and has exhibited in Canada, the Netherlands, and Czechia. He divides his time between Field, British Columbia, and Amsterdam. A selected writings is appearing shortly.

Streetcar Out, Owl's Claw In

*Poetry exists somewhere between order and chaos, thriving
on both: sometimes providing an orderly sequence, sometimes
giving us mere fluttering of thought blown around the page.*
— Anne Simpson, *The Marram Grass: Poetry & Otherness*

Birds, Pity Nostradamus

Domine, forgive me my memories — a strange
thought to enter the snail of the head.

An old man makes soup much like a child would, if only
to tolerate the afternoons. And cleans himself with candles.

Months or years, feel the fish-cold stone. The first of night's
flagships is a kitchen's worn-down floor.

Birds, pity Nostradamus, locked into the future, and
forced to write its fierceness down.

Writing isn't tennis, isn't a star's vacant steps, isn't a table
one face deep. It's a collection of missing fingerprints.

But the past is, the past is, the past is an enclosure,
a change room only a few of us have ever seen.

And new love/she's wearing smiling skulls on her finest boxers,
never, never to cradle suicide's astonished microphone.

Yes, words really do

dream   maintains Gaston Bachelard.
You are so lucky   to be young.

      (To fall asleep the next night, I returned to my old strategy of
          picturing the whole world flooding inch by inch.
— Daniel Sherrell, *Warmth: Coming of Age at the End of Our World*

Because the future undresses
the sunlight with dirty fingernails, each of us
must tell at least
         somebody's
memoirs —)
           — If he'd   lift his eyes
the crucified Jesus on Charles Bridge in Prague would take
in the tourists being photographed by each other
as a woman runs past to grasp
the two clusters of bronze leaves
beneath his feet as she
         prays for at least a minute
and then steps back to where her white-shirted husband's waiting,
  reaches
up, and holds his cheeks. Jesus is dark with centuries
of grime but the leaves are shiny
     from those passersby who
come out of the crowd
to touch them. And not far
from this bridge, Hermann
Kafka sleeps and Hermann
Göring shields his face
with his hand   from
the Russian photographer at the Nuremberg
Trials. Hides his face only from
      the Russian. Yanks and Brits can flash
away, but to the Russian:
        Nihil. These, then,
are dedications to Yevgeny Khaldei who was never

paid but keeps showing up during the Olympics
while protesters might
be permitted to demonstrate at theme
and amusement parks, near
the outskirts of Beijing. Everyone

2.
feel free
to drop by: discover what concerns us: words
                                        outside of anyone's
ability to choose. Decide between a parking lot or
a porcelain, tubercular cup. Keep learning that our time
together isn't simply an experiment. Simply
the way it bruises beneath

and overtop this insensible
subtraction, the very bridge

that stares back from any
object
        made with the hands. Such enormous
things
can sometimes happen.

3.
And then they do.

What Do I Owe the Clock beside the Bed?

A half hour of karaoke, and the weight
of a leopard's tail. Pure
                    autumn.
This morning, just down
the path, a man's
                    carrying, not walking
beside, his venereal
shadow. Overtop
a concert of buried
grass, myopic, scarred bricks, the goodness
of abandoned windows
and toil —

Life is three children perplexed by their grandfather's
lawn ornaments, his glowing face
alongside the lake —

And what
is owed

my daughter, my sons? They've
                    made
a sandcastle, and then ask
if lightning

will kill it *eventually*.

Second Worlds

Stare; pry; listen; eavesdrop. Die knowing something.
You are not here long.
— Walker Evans

I'm writing a treatise on anger. On
what's   light. A disquisition learned / from
        (amidst)
what this photograph incites:

First, just above her heavy belt of stars, you see this: letters spelling
unlovable tattooed on her lower back. Her little boy, their joined
hands. Head tilted — he's learning to watch for cars. And who comes
toward him. The replayed and various world. His baseball cap nearly
covering his blond head. In Gothic lettering on her shoulder bag the
words: **love, baby, language**. There's another tattoo, a star, this one
on her right arm, the one holding his hand. You will never see their
faces. And how does anyone read the contemptuous amphitheater
of her skin, its urgent

and undecided permanence? Its (unquenched) anger. Just as,
right now, you see there's abruptly nothing beyond the lips
a song a decade once left behind, there's not even carefully
betrayed love / there's just a blank branch upon
which a magpie once sat. I point my
                                eyes into this inaudible flood, and then
listen because all that's capable of motion in the waiting and
     unpreventable
world is within earshot.   Replay everything
twice. The little boy will discover how
the mind can't even once be remembered.

2.
I'm writing a treatise on rage. On grief. A sea lion
blinded by gunshot. Rage and grief, they travel
separately to form what a century leaves
on the sky's polished black sand. Watch

my son, furious with me, as I wash his small
hands in mine before he eats his pizza. He feels himself
by feeling the enclosing others. Burn it all down, he means, burn
everything fucking down. Easy now. You must be patient. Anger
doesn't let just anyone in. Study Saint Francis

Bacon. Study our passage into tomorrow's jet-
        lagged meat. Study alongside the very old. They shape nouns
                differently: purse   hip   shoes   memory.   Fingers
Bathtub.   Television.   Christopher Columbus was wrong: the
        world is

3.
flat. Look at your life: nothing returns. The world is a burning toy:
at its edge, millions and millions of photographs, each
of someone somebody loved, a waterfall of them, going over
the edge and down into forever, down into what's gone. And in
        between
only a few with zombie rage & fewer even care to try riding
this one out, try tattooing some feathers onto our skin, only a few —

4.
Little is as forgiving as space: you can walk a long time
within the eye's fingertip, though no one has ever
learned how to live inside what the eye can hold.

You keep vanishing.

But the world can do anything it wants on a dance floor — if there's
        enough darkness
outside. And when I die, I want you to take a wine glass and break it
        against
what night ignores, its quick continent of roughened cloud
                                        & if the oldest
of Persephone's skies won't shatter the glass, then my fury
will have been warranted.

5.

She once sat amidst all of this: my daughter. Posing behind a pair of glasses bought from a circus. And when I take her picture, she's moved her hands, palm next to palm together, as if pretending to pray. For everything. Her dress restrained behind a tangle of buttons. Behind her, more photos on the closed door. Her mother once reading a novel in a washroom in an American motel. Another woman, this one has three blurred feet dancing across a courtyard in the rain. Just then, when I saw her, I stepped aside from my life for a day. But that was enough —

I'm writing a treatise about being forever surprised. Each week
      someone
sends me candles. They scatter pieces of what my senses once
knew. It's not Wednesday, a word which, when
said slowly, is as beautiful as the yellow-headed
blackbird that's turning the street
                              upside down when
                  it flies up from a puddle
            because something
         is approaching.
                  A car, or a dog,
or
simply a kid on a rusty bike. And you hold
the tattooed woman
                  her hips / from behind / and ask her
what do you want to do
tomorrow? The gentlest
words

in our language.

Streetcar Out, Owl's Claw In: Some Notes on Lyric Poetry

Lyric poets try to articulate the blind universe that passes through everyone.

Obsessed with transience, lyric poems unwrap immediacy with undiscovered combinations of words. They rebel against time and the daily blur of what happens. While poems probe and often celebrate the nature of the present — the present, that amazing glue to which nothing sticks — they also manifest a radical skepticism, accentuating how little we know about anything.

Put differently, lyric poetry enacts the war between what's visible and the amplitude of what's missing.

I find composition to be entirely baffling. It took almost two years to round out "The Colour White Begins" but maybe four hours for "Birds, Pity Nostradamus." Regardless of the time it takes to write a poem, the images that show up engage in a kind of slow drift. The Nostradamus poem, a kind of undisciplined ghazal, started with a tabloid article I saw in a grocery store. When I began the poem, I had no idea it would end, an afternoon later, recalling a woman I loved who killed herself in the mid-1980s. Reading the completed poem, I realize that the final line was inevitable after the first couplet was written. During composition the mind may open itself to abandoned memories and perceptions, but that doesn't mean a poem charts this interior process. There's an image that was originally part of "The Colour White": an overturned streetcar. I don't know where the image came from; it just popped into my head. The streetcar strongly insisted on being in the poem, persisting through many drafts, but then I cut it because it seemed too idiosyncratic, too narrowly personal (though I've never seen a streetcar lying on its side). So, I left the image out and went on to other things. But some time later, I came across a photo in a newspaper commemorating the 1956 revolution in Hungary — and there was the precise overturned streetcar. I wasn't alive in 1956 to see the original news image, so I must have encountered it later as a child. I remembered none of these historical details when I worked on the poem. The image simply presented itself, and then the exigencies of the poem that wanted to be written took over: streetcar out, owl's claw in. But I like to think that somewhere, hovering just beyond or beneath the page, is an homage to the exact defiance that caused people to riot in Budapest in 1956.

The Edges of What's Known?

I've been drinking a piano's terrible whisky since
We keep losing how newly it is to be temporary,
dawn, fleeing your anger from before our lives began.

Toward me, toward her, toward the rocky south of the bed, she
the blind universe passing through everyone, seeking asylum
touches herself with the sunburned fingers of her right hand.

Slow dance a skeleton's returning slumber; wait; the taxis
from each laggard lifetime, unwrapping immediacy from
line up outside the bright balance of what happens.

She signs off her emails *fingertips,* an eyelid from
a cluster of faces and the pale wilds of skin, the flickering
Kafka's incurable time when people sent postcards.

The edges of what's known? A child's sandals, the burst
shore adrift from somewhere back then, we retain so little:
of weather and hatred. Are we just friends? Sirens.

The loosening skin of forgiveness taking decades
either there's nothing worth keeping or nothing that
to learn. And never once, the words *delightful déjà vu,* cut

from a guidebook and taped on your bathroom
can be kept, our lives don't live within us that way —
mirror for a selfie that no one's ever seen before.

Decoy

Poetry is an artifact of the world that has ended.
— Michael Robbins, "A Conversation about Trees"

Hard to disagree. An extinct wordivore. An improvised glass
sutra sodden as Mylar's hybridity but inert. As shape-shifting

as unintended original sin. Therefore nothing, really. Therefore
now becoming a hobby store–rocket word that stalls mid-air

incandescent

in the simple science of lighting the birthday candle world.
Fancy recitations. Conceits. This excavating the birthday candle

world wearing a life that's too big too small on each of us
renovating ↔ conjuring ↔ summoning ↔ evacuating

nothing, really. A grindhouse   a wavelength   a very difficult
a cannot properly   a mismatched   a dear   gesture   a
                                                    lure

A Single Pair of Eyeglasses

I once said that after Auschwitz one could no longer write poetry, and that gave rise to a discussion I did not anticipate when I wrote those words. I did not anticipate it because it is in the nature of philosophy — and everything I write is, unavoidably, philosophy, even if it is not concerned with so-called philosophical themes — that nothing is meant quite literally.

— Theodor W. Adorno, *Metaphysics: Concept and Problems*

Clio

The artist only skims off the most fleeting appearance of
reality, only brushes it, in order then to swing free of all reality.
The historian on the other hand is interested only
in reality and must search its depths.
— Wilhelm von Humboldt, "On the Task of the Historian"

If you could only look behind today
you'd find a pair of good black shoes

staring from a courtyard. This is yesterday's
self-portrait, its sudden inheritance

of disbelief. If only we could look behind
today's meagre widening, its nearby sun

that keeps strip-mining the present; if only we
could retrace what's kept between distance

and disaster. But we

2.
populate a raw kingdom
and whenever you —

whenever anyone — looks
for her, Clio strikes

a match and we all
go missing.

Aristotle initiates one of his inquiries by

noting that it's through vision that people most delight in knowing —

— Have I said it before? I am learning to see. Yes, I am beginning. It's still going badly. But I intend to make the most of my time.
     — Rainer Maria Rilke, *The Notebooks of Malte Laurids Brigge*

— I had to see everything. I had to watch hour after hour, by day and by night, the removal and burning of the bodies, the extraction of the teeth, the cutting of the hair, the whole grisly, interminable business […] I had to stand for hours on end […] I had to look through the peep-hole of the gas chambers and watch the process of death itself, because the doctors wanted me to see it.
     — Rudolf Höss, *Commandant of Auschwitz:*
     The Autobiography of Rudolf Höss

— I look around me: incapacity to experience the present. This cool-ness, this thinness, this calm and collected busyness. Our eyes are turned inward. Our visual faculty is unequal to the reality we inhabit. There ought to be something in us that makes us realize the image becomes permanent the moment we take it in. Right now it is thin, fluid, might just as well not be there.
     — David Koker, *At the Edge of the Abyss: A Concentration Camp Diary, 1943–1944*

— At Auschwitz and Birkenau themselves, the truth is there for all to see, and to see is better to understand.
     — Leon Greenman, *An Englishman in Auschwitz*

Greenman's wife Else & his son Barney were wearing

clothes that she'd sewn from velvet curtains, red capes that he could make out from a distance in the truck beneath a searchlight that separated them from the others

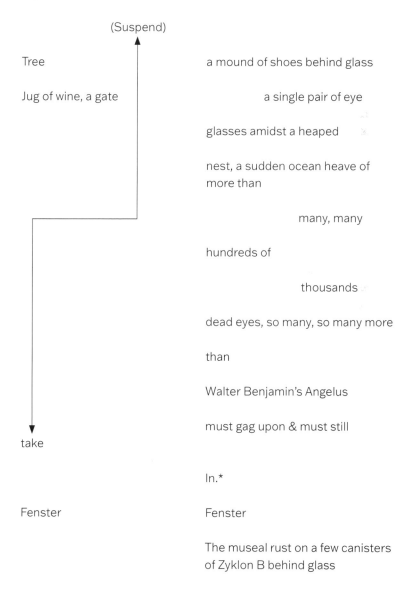

(Suspend)

Tree   a mound of shoes behind glass

Jug of wine, a gate   a single pair of eye

glasses amidst a heaped

nest, a sudden ocean heave of
more than

many, many

hundreds of

thousands

dead eyes, so many, so many more

than

Walter Benjamin's Angelus

must gag upon & must still

take

In.*

Fenster   Fenster

The museal rust on a few canisters
of Zyklon B behind glass

53

Unready Nouns

*The Paul Klee drawing Benjamin once owned — its precise childlike warning/accusation only clear when you see it across the gallery, watching you from a piece of old and very ordinary, slightly browned paper — was on display in Boston's Museum of Fine Arts from the summer of 2012 to early January 2013 as part of the Ori Gersht exhibit. Presumably, the Angel had been returned to its glass case in Jerusalem when two bombs went off at the Boston Marathon only a few months later.

Paradise:
the response given by Wilfred von Oven, Joseph Goebbels's personal assistant, upon being asked, in 1990, how he might summarize his experience of the Third Reich in one word.

An email written to SL from Amsterdam on Wednesday, November 16, 2011

Have walked around quite a bit today beneath lovely grey skies, bits of rain, first the Rijksmuseum, and then just general flâneurie, a chat with my wife, and did my laundry; nice to have fresh clothes when you're travelling. Then walked around some more. It makes sense that the Dutch started NYC becos the two cities seem to have much in common in terms of their odd light, general sort of free-for-all on the streets, and tolerant excess.

Yesterday I rented a car and drove to Westerbork (the transit camp the Nazis used to send over 101,000 people, mostly Jews, to Poland's camps), but I won't describe it just now except to say that there's a museum re: Nazism (attended yesterday by a class of schoolchildren caught up in their own games), but then you need to walk a little under 4km to get to the camp. You follow a zigzaggy brick path amidst this most beautiful forest, and all along the walkway are these enormous discoloured green satellite dishes lined up in the clearings, and pictures [along the walkway] showing the universe because this area is where Holland has its largest gatherings of radio telescopes. So here's a snapshot of our species: the way we educate our young, the 1940s, and we reach to discover more about the universe: tell me about this creature responsible for all of these things.

Something that was unexpected is how beautiful these places are in the autumn. While in Poland, I went to Auschwitz twice, and both times was in Birkenau at dusk, which comes early amidst enormous trees, some of which must have been there when the camp was in use. At one point during my first afternoon there, it thundered, and it took me a moment to realise it was thundering because I've always associated such weather with a mood of quiet excitement, joy. Thunder didn't feel normal there. What did it mean for inmates to hear something from their previous lives that was as normal and exciting as a storm approaching? Did it even register for them? How? How could they comprehend what was on the other side of their lives, what was entirely separate from them? Something that surprised me: people have put cigarette butts in the small stoves in the surviving barracks and there are dozens of names carved into the wooden walls and bunks. (Note: these aren't from the 1940s; they're from recent tourists.)

Such a change, then, to come to Amsterdam and look at Rembrandt, Vermeer, Steen. Looking at paintings, the retina takes an undiluted image straight to the brain, but the brain doesn't have to subdue what the eye sees, filter it, and then somehow re-imagine, somehow overlay what's directly in front of you with what's missing as it does in Auschwitz or Westerbork. I spent a long time looking at a simple picture Rembrandt made of an old woman reading, and he devotes all of his genius at painting her wrinkled, aging hand that's resting on the enormous book. I bought a plastic reproduction, but it can't convey the paper feel of her almost gecko/like skin. There: in front of yr eyes, is something he made only a few centuries ago. I don't think I've ever seen any representation that more fully embodies the human than her hand.

It's very strange, then, to leave these paintings and walk south on the Museumplein for a few minutes to Gabriël Metsustraat 6, which is where Etty Hillesum lived during part of the war. There's a plaque at street level identifying this place as her residence, but the dates it gives, oddly, are incorrect. She once wrote about looking out her window toward the Rijksmuseum which, in the mist, seemed to be a "turreted city far away." But the plaque's all that's there now — unlike the Anne Frank House, this row house is still someone's home — and I didn't notice anyone stop to read what was written there alongside the doorway.

Warmly to you, from that other city with canals.

PS Find attached a photo taken at Westerbork yesterday.

Today, I turned a corner in Amsterdam's Joods Historisch Museum and unexpectedly saw some notebooks in a glass case. There were only five of them, but I sensed immediately that they must have been Etty's. Because there were no identifying labels, I couldn't be sure until I finally found a computer display that worked and touched the icon that identified the stack of ringed notebooks as being hers.

On August 31, 1943, the Tuesday before Etty's transport, Philip Mechanicus recorded how "loathsome" it was that ballet dancers were ordered to rehearse their routine for an upcoming theatrical show while that week's transport was being readied and then sent east, Gemmeker having committed 2,000 guilders to pay for costumes.

The American pelicans are going to disappear

from the creek soon but should return in a few months before heading south for the winter. Their wingtips the colour of the four crows chastising an unleashed dog in the park. A woman eating an ice cream cone just rode past on a bicycle. And (then a father goes by explaining evolution to his youngest daughter who's riding shotgun on his shoulders.
— Diary notes: June 4, 2010)

The sky's the colour of a cognac (bottled the year Napoleon invaded Russia) offered to guests on the *Graf Zeppelin* on its 1929 flight around the world, the alcohol a gift from a connoisseur living in Berlin.

Not all spiders make webs.

A definition of metaphysics: my eldest son, then aged six: Dad, I'd like to try being someone else. I want to be other people. I could even be a piece of furniture.

A picnic life.

Having lunch with a friend who has this lovely habit of turning his body sideways when he laughs. He's telling me Bergman films manifest forgiveness through light…when we both get brain freeze. What's the name of Bergman's central male actor?

A perfectly clear sentence that cannot be understood today.

A demonstration of three-dimensional irony:

I can remember how my son stood just beyond the kitchen, in the living room by the aquarium — this was in early July, 2005 — and I'm fairly certain that we were getting ready to go swimming. I'd been divorced from his mom for a bit over a year and was keeping a lookout for signs of adjustment problems. Both my kids with her, he and his older sister, were with me for a week while she attended a conference on urban literature in London, England.

"The Bitter War over Anne Frank's Soul": title of a 1997 newspaper article describing how the Anne Frank House "shamed a Spanish company into dropping plans for Anne Frank jeans."

Because when Lady Hay Drummond-Hay wired the sentence about the picnic life to the Hearst newspaper employing her, she meant not that the culinary offerings on the *Graf Zeppelin* were festive, but that they had to be utterly simple, almost rustic, owing to logistical problems of space and weight.

Alchemy over juxtaposition.

Vindobona.

Daniel Pearl was the journalist.

Where Marcus Aurelius died in 180; now called Vienna.

That near Westerbork, where once lived a Neolithic people who left a gathering of stones on the heath. Etty Hillesum's desire, expressed nearby in 1942, to someday visit everyone who passed through the transit camp on their way east. To see each of them, one by one, with her own eyes.

How one remembers certain things is beyond me.

Shot in the jaw while participating in the Sobibór revolt on October 14, 1943, at age sixteen.

Michael Herr realising, after five minutes of abstruse conversation with a sergeant drinking a beer at the NCO club, that the man had been on duty for days during the Tet Offensive and was somehow deeply asleep standing there.

Tomasz "Toivi" Blatt, who renamed himself Thomas Blatt, who succumbed to dementia in Santa Barbara, seventy-two years after Sobibór.

Five babies born the year Gauguin died: Theodor W. Adorno, Joseph Cornell, Walker Evans, Lou Gehrig, Mark Rothko —

Ordinary terror.

1903.

Where life makes sense.

Name of twenty-first-century luxury cruise ship especially designed to navigate the shallow seas of French Polynesia, with seventy per cent of cabins having private balconies. Guess.

The sign on the Trans-Canada Highway that welcomes visitors into Swift Current, Saskatchewan.

Marcel Duchamp, photographed by Duane Michals in 1964, on the wall to the left.

2010.

A parable about historical transmission.

Year in which Anne Frank House announces its permission for a graphic biography to be made of her life (1929–45).

Wondering if she remembered another news report she sent, this time by carrier pigeon, describing the exuberant reception of the *Zeppelin* in Tokyo, when she died a decade and a half later in New York, after being incarcerated for three years in a Japanese prison camp for civilians.

For a few moments this light on the screen comes from a place devoid of anything that could bring harm into the world.

Look at the Pacific: nothing could save you if you fell. But you're not falling. Not a single person in the history of our species has experienced what you're feeling…just now. And no one other than you ever will.

Let the cognac ignite your eyes.

Sitting in Washington Square in the autumn of 2009, having just walked from St. Paul's, across from Ground Zero, and about to visit the nearby drugstore Joseph Cornell once frequented to get material for his shadow boxes.

For all of us who come after.

No photography permitted by order of the owner.

(An elegy for David Markson)

Disneyland

Waiting a few hours at Chicago's O'Hare airport, sitting nearby one of its myriad overhead TVs, I watched CNN continually announce that a young American from Minnesota had been killed as a jihadi in Syria. The eternal loop of the new. Ostensibly to provide background about numerous other Americans who had become radicalized and subsequently left Minnesota, the news station replayed an older recruitment video showing a young man smiling, shortly before he, too, was killed. Entirely relaxed in front of the camera, grinning, ebullient, he reveals:

This is the real
Disneyland —
              jihad overseas that is, Mr. Troy K. lets us know. He's
finally flourishing
in a recruitment video shown back home. *This is the real Disneyland,*
      if you guys
only knew. He's
                  a pixelated Achilles from Minneapolis, a lion with only
      one tooth
missing, just having fun, surfing destiny's
                              avalanche, belonging
forever to irony swerving into more
irony and defunct.

It was a tragedy, a mother tells a reporter —

Aristotle suffers his hand to rest
on Homer's original skull:
we're all outlaws
now —

2.
Especially
           this man: he's holding grocery bags
against a lineup of four specifically shadowed tanks,
                                    though the postcard
I bought in Vienna, twenty-five years and forty-four days after
Tiananmen, shows a single tank trailing a bar code now that
    memory's
nobody's playlist, a latent ratio
measuring   active oblivion: chance. Where
is Tank Man and is he well? Well and where? And how is
it that time is scrubbed clean of what
                              happens? And what's meant
for listening now
                    that images are instant
and failed migrations?

Watch Garry Winogrand's falling
man in New York tumble from   (the Δ Shirtwaist Factory)
the 1950s to 9/11 just as
                    the towers' jumpers
land back
         in the Stroop Report (that Adolf Eichmann held intact
in his hands), showing Warsaw's rebels leap from burning buildings
in 1943.   Adolf Eichmann?

Just beneath the Salztorbrücke in Vienna — rebuilt after the
war — there's a wide pathway along the Danube Canal. On both sides
of the water, there are high embankments the city sets aside for
graffiti. Standing on the bridge, looking down, I watched a young man
unzip a backpack to remove a gas mask and proceed to spray a kind
of Kandinsky space-scape overtop somebody else's tag. He didn't see
me and seemed to be in a hurry, which surprised me because others
had taken the time to create careful panels up and down both sides
of the canal. His tattooed arm was a hummingbird with a spray can.
Soon he packed up, sprinted off on his bicycle, unpaid and nostalgic,
leaving behind whatever swift adjustments an artist might offer to

weather and the various passersby. Comparing him to a hummingbird is to start with what the mind knows

innocently, to ungas a removing
mask, to gather an instant
abundance that is then
threatened when

you look back across the Franz-Josefs-Kai (Ringstrasse) to the large building on the corner of the intersection. Earlier, I'd been following a map to locate the city's monument dedicated to the "Victims of Fascism." When I found it, abandoned in the welcome shadows of trees, I was taken by how small, claustrophobic, and jarringly modernist it is. Damp. The building across the street from the memorial had a barely observable frieze on its second-floor balcony showing a noose, a guillotine, and a man sprawled across barbed wire. The numerals MCMXXXVIII and MCMXXXXV were carved at either end of the frieze. I went into a skateboarding store that was on the ground floor of what was obviously an apartment building above and asked a clerk about the frieze. This young man accompanied me outside and told me that guidebooks claiming the memorial in the park across the street was built upon the site where the Gestapo had their headquarters were wrong: the actual offices had been where we stood, but it was bombed and this new building replaced it. Apparently, the Gestapo had secured this location shortly after the Nazis invaded Austria. I noticed his use of the word *invaded* and asked him if Adolf Eichmann had ever had an office in the building. Lighting a cigarette, taking a break from the shop, he apologized that he didn't recognize the name.

What neither he nor I knew is that the building the Gestapo confiscated from its Jewish owners was the Hotel Métropole, and the Gestapo bureau in Vienna was larger than the one in Berlin, employing around nine hundred staff. Approximately fifty thousand enemies of the Reich had been summoned to the newly refurbished luxury hotel before the Allies bombed it, destroying its Corinthian columns, caryatids, and Atlases, whose fleshless exertions wouldn't be needed anymore.

We delight in imitation, says Aristotle to Dutch children using an old
umbrella to play
paratrooper after the Nazi Blitzkrieg in the first spring of the war.

3.
It's not
that beauty's
stalled
over the grave that evil's
made —
        it's that revolt has
nowhere to go and can
leave nothing
abiding in
its place.

4.
Opening day for the renovated Field Museum in Chicago, May 21, 1921, a line of hundreds (mostly darkly dressed adults wearing hats), moving across a stone-littered field toward one of the museum's entrances, engineered with Ionic columns; inside are seventeen acres of uncorroded natural history made available that sunless morning for the first time:

It's so rare that anything happens for the first time, Clio reminds herself, closing her eyes in Vermeer's studio, the restless light just about to fall asleep on her unpredictable lips —

A man stopping in front of King Jagiełło's statue in New York's Central Park tells his son on October 30, 2009 — "They're still pissed off about something that happened in 1410…that's what most of these monuments are for" — and then the pair heads home, crossing a few of the park's thirty-six bridges, while in Poland the massive forest Jagiełło set aside for hunting still contains oaks from his reign, trees that nature buff Hermann Göring once sectioned off for his private use; this forest is the only remaining place in which each of the nine species of European woodpecker continues to survive. But just before I eavesdropped on these people, I'd seen a plaque on a park bench not far from the statue that had the following commemoration:

In loving memory of Linda C. Lee
7.22.67 to 9.11.01
A thing of beauty is a joy forever;
Its loveliness increases; It will never
Pass into nothingness.

And only today, the *New York Times* records the stories of two women: one is Africa's only female billionaire (made wealthy by oil) and the other has buried ten of her fifteen children and her only experience with gasoline is when she uses it to rinse her mouth to anaesthetize the pain incurred by her rotting and devastated teeth. In Andrzej Wajda's *Korczak*, the actor playing

the title character declares: "Describing the suffering of others is like a theft. As if we hadn't enough misery already." In the film, rescue is both sure and denied. Emptying a bucket of piss into the street and closing a door behind the night in this scene, he refuses to admonish what remains of the future.

5.
When Marcus Aurelius looks at his reflection
	You must look at zombies with kindness
He sees standing behind him a figure with a sculptured
	When you say peekaboo! and then fire
Mind just like his own, a radiant spectator who, taking pleasure
	Away, now that nature and Himmler
In the cypresses, feels part of the whole, someone who remains
	Have imparted their secrets: just what
Unsurprised by coarse and violent men, and maintains
	Would Jesus do? Kein mitleid
Unconcern when oblivion returns as each morning's
	No mercy as apparitional
		Evidence.
		Evidence.

6.
When he got dressed that day, this aging man with the dark
suit jacket, he didn't know that he'd turn
onto
Vinohradská Avenue to find his gaze
suddenly fixed by a stranger's
					camera. For that second perhaps
it seemed there was	something happening apart
from the chaos and disbelief and	what remains
of his face today is a gelatin silver print shown

in a Josef Koudelka exhibit in Chicago,
the negative
having been smuggled away from Prague
with its spurned and untenable tanks
forty-six years before when the Warsaw
Pact liberators invaded Praha —

Today's Angelus Novus, this man, he's old enough
to have seen people sent away
					to Terezin, and possibly

heard about the absorbent mattresses
slumped against a wall in Lidice fast upon
Heydrich's death…and months after

   (this month, Yeshi Khando, a nun,
     immolated herself to protest Chinese
     rule, the 138th Tibetan to do so since
       2009)

this picture was taken in '68 he would learn of Jan
Palach. That is, if he was still alive
then, but we can know
nothing of this man.
                              Returning
to his image often, taken in by his posture, his need to walk
through his city, to show himself   amidst disarray, I wonder
if he washed his own shirts, ever covered a book he was
reading with brown paper so an informer on a streetcar couldn't
report him, whether he enjoyed shaving. Over the irresistible
     decades
this man behind glass holds two ordinary words: confront…retains.
And this man with the soft, crumpled shirt, this aging man hidden
behind his metamorphic eyebrows and forehead and something
that got scorched   that day, he cautions me not to content myself
too quickly with my own definitions of the unknowable.

7.
The moment each child detects the miracle: there's
someone inside me
                         that no one
else can see?

Three old friends, retirees in Orlando, Florida, sipping a finely chilled
Nachträglichkeit, T.W. Adorno, Simone de Beauvoir, and Sigmund
Freud, discuss the newest female doll on the market: its cutting-
edge technology allowing the toy to maintain an actual (interactive)
conversation with a child in real time, which is transmitted (over Wi-Fi)
simultaneously to the parent

company for analysis amidst irony side-swiping
irony and night's astonished lullaby, a neon-black

hot-air balloon shaped like a flamingo adrift and
exacting, adrift and implacably drifting over

the uniforms and crowds below: it's not
only your own life you're squandering.

Unscathed

Dear Selection Committee:

If words are clay, then let me try
disaster's opposite:
a child's scrapbook.

Please pay fucking attention children. There are only
three rooms left along the river. Beneath
the ice, water making its way over scraps
of dead lightning. The sky
sewing
                one patch of something
onto another —

Can I ever leave this place my mother's dreamed?
Three things, maybe five: a bit of snail quartz, a turmeric cloud, what.
    The hand

keeps wanting
to   hold:
        (how beautiful is beautiful if forgetting isn't the same
for everyone?) A shot glass filled with a cockatoo's blood. Father, can
    you
keep what can't be kept from wild & shining
snow, from what's*

2.
dissolved into what everything one day becomes?

*Vermeer in Terezin: What happened when children there in art class
copied Vermeer's painting of a man sharing some wine with a woman,
and they cut up pieces of felt to then collage together, something to
make something alongside of: a diamond floor and what no one can
know: for many of these children the three dates now preserved in the

Pinkas Synagogue in Praha: when they were born + when they arrived
in Terezin + and when: almost…all of them: Auschwitz-Birkenau.

You keep moving to the back because it's not only your clothes that
stink.

If Robert Frank's forgotten and celebrated photograph *Trolley — New
Orleans* is the accident of an eyelid, then both light and Rosa Parks will
never be disturbed. A photograph starts out by showing a streetcar in
New Orleans, call it the late 1950s, a time when no one should ever
have to spend a life working if only just to die. The rule of

thirds: our first landscape remains the face and its sway
between hunger
                delight
and harm.

The Mountains Are Hallucinating

The sublime is so alone. It watches us.
  — Jorie Graham, *Fast*

The Mountains

are hallucinating again, this time
a bright cluster of pumpkins in the snow.

The river's litter of stones
are long past midnight —

as someone lays out breakfast dishes only
a few hours from the day's delivery

of flowers freshly cut in Kenya.
Tomorrow's roses are
                              flying now, a fence length of children
                                        flying
toward (unstriped) white linen in Berlin.

It's not that most things are hard to describe that's disturbing —
watching the stones beneath the Bow River after the first snow, or
hearing a waiter lay out plates and cutlery, keeping to himself, doing
a task that must've been performed by so many others each night for
decades in this Berlin hotel — what's worrisome is something else,
something beyond a friend's grave illness, something that I sense but
can't quite discern:

And now,
          only five years later, my hearing's going: I could see, but not
     hear, the

Baltimore oriole's sudden slash, its plumage an orange
that only it has; nowhere other than on
its belly does this orange
                              stay: an atheist in a crowd of
believers.

Two Letters
To the colour grey

I never noticed the colour grey until the afternoon I learned that I didn't understand tides. A teenager from southern Ontario, I'd been hiking along the rocky shore of northern California, encountering tide pools for the first time, and then exploring a sea cave. Sat inside it for an hour, but then it began to fill with water. It hadn't occurred to me that tides could go so high. Or arrive so quickly. I had to swim back to the forest trailhead that had emptied onto the beach, struggling to hold my binoculars above the waves.

Before it began raining hard, a flock of pelicans flying up and down the beach, clearly at play.

The sky turned dark, and it's taken me years to understand that seeing all those greys jostling between clouds, falling rain, and waves was perhaps the moment in my life that I was furthest from any kind of anxiety, sadness, or distress. Overcast skies still soothe. I wouldn't see that precise mixture of colour until years later, when I gave my first serious girlfriend a birthday present for the first time: some brushes and oils, and three taut canvases. Her ambition then was to become a painter, and she squeezed some fresh paint from the tube, smeared a line inside her forearm to see if it was the tint she imagined.

I fell for both of them, of course — the woman and the colour — the paint a kind of grey blue I've loved for over forty years, though I can't remember what it's called. Stores selling house paint place it somewhere close to Myriad Oceans or Vermont Slate, but I've never seen anyone get it right, this colour striving to become something else: on the one end of its spectrum it wants to be a child's finger on the trigger of a shiny toy gun; on the other, a spade turning over earth while digging a vegetable garden.

There's a house a few snowy alleys from here, a kind of pigeon-moored grey, with a silver horse head gracing each peak of the roof, one facing an oblique east, the other curved toward a pine, dark as river silt in the night's remaining hour, the nearly green moon humming just now like a glow-in-the-dark dinosaur.

To my first love, and every possible future we haven't met together.

Another birthday has come and here we are in late middle age, me sending an email across the Atlantic to touch on our separate lives. One, two, three, four marriages ago (divided equally between us), I gave you some art supplies. I don't know if you remember them or even paint anymore.

If we'd managed to find a few bare minutes this year I'd have offered some cold Viognier and reminded you of when we stood in front of Adriaen Coorte's bunch of asparagus, the uncrowded light gliding along its stems.

If I could say something to my younger self, I'd mention two things that I've only recently learned: that a man's wife had to carry their hidden helping of a few asparagus stalks in wartime Dresden because it was a *pure* Aryan vegetable and the Gestapo would arrest her Jewish husband for simply touching them; and that twenty-seven thousand years earlier, someone's holding a child's hand in the Gargas Caves and blowing ancient paint over the skin. This is gentleness dwelling at one end and fear at another, not things I thought much about, back then.

...

But jealousy I knew, that unimaginable addiction, that blindfold pressed closer than waking up tomorrow, before you took it with you, jealousy I mean, rolled it up like a worn poster and mailed it so far into the uncreased future that it took twenty years alongside one wife and two kids before the tube arrived and inside was a stranger who rode into our world on a bicycle with handlebars so wide she compared them to the horns of a water buffalo. She's the one upstairs in the room beside our own son's, as they sleep their way along the separate and unintelligible hallways that measure our lives — sometimes with the slow motion of leniency, sometimes with unfastened brutality — and one of my eyes is aching, which leaves my defenses down, so I shut them both to the drone of an incoming plane that feels so near it's shaving the side of my face that's complaining and now even more memory arrives, unlived, sudden like a single runway instantly shining beneath the prairie's dark.

Meanwhile the climate's gone wrong. Some Bohemian waxwings have returned, too early to flock on yesterday's trees, their voices the grinding of small wires casting brightness across the hoarfrost, a tamarack's thin branches showing buds of frozen basmati rice, each grain but one part of every possible future we haven't met together, though I keep returning to how you've taught your sons that when people in broken boats appear during a picnic on the Spanish beach, they must be given the dry towels and what there is to eat, and you must push them into a crowd so they disappear when the civil guard comes searching, and you must always say no, no, you haven't seen anything at all.

Three young men, each holding a lobster

in front of his belly, promenade around Wascana Lake (six claws
closed in three different rubber bands: blue, green &
an abbreviated orange)…each of them
                                    wanting to:
                                                dirty up
the day's cummerbund making joyful indeed, thank you —

Thank you, young men, for keeping drained-dry-as-sparkles
rebellious
and rejecting
verity. Let's all of us welcome too, what's called a flock
of
    ruddy ducks skittish
about to take off from the lake, creatures whose brains
can allocate one eye

        independently

to look nearby   to scan distance
for food   for predators

---

the wind as a bridge and a silhouette of ganglia

separate from us.   Our drift.   The blue of the male

ruddy duck's bills a pigment
                            most people have seen
only once before: on the headgear used by
the UN when it's a soldier peacekeeping on TV and
                            today there's so much flooding in the Balkans
that   untold

numbers of abandoned land mines have been coughed up and are
    dead/swimming
toward hydroelectric dams only so far down from the unrepentant

        blur
of here —

2.
When does a detail neither thicken nor dissolve into an example?

3.
The Nazis (I'm beginning to learn
have ruined everything. No, I keep learning
that they) keep staining everything. Christ, I'd thought
that a few things were safe: the turning flash of white
on a kingbird's tail, the yellow no one anywhere
has ever been able
                to rename that's
around a pelican's unpebbled eye, but no, they keep showing up
everywhere: Hermann Langbein telling me last night of:

Professor Günther Niethammer, who, awarded the unusual job by
the SS of watching birds in the marshes surrounding Auschwitz-
Birkenau, didn't deny what was done to inmates, but he moved his
lookout tower so he could study birds without having to look at what
happened away from him.

I need to know, I need to know at least two things
from you, Herr Doctor Niethammer: at what point does
a detail from your life become an example, become something
that might instruct us in perceiving everything

in what isn't here for you:
and second:

(http://onlinelibrary.wiley.com/doi/10.1111/j.1474-919X.1975
    .tb04230.x/pdf)

what would you advise us to do?

Always See the Bigger Picture

And for fun, pick up, download the almost
uncanny microscope app: point it at your skin
down beneath the fading tats to see the mistakes
collagen eventually makes → here alongside
                           the lively bacteria chattering
               inside this new Southern Gothic thing
this fade-away-in-real-time my disinherited
                           decades long ago chose to become. So soon
                           the body hosts an honestly virulent
                                          and festive agitation
          in the limestone caves
          of these disintegrating
          lungs. This singular heart.
          Nerves as memory fraying as an
          elderly child's tingling peripheral
          neuropathy. No matter.
                           Decide
          between the autumn world where the derelict
          and fiercely intellectual sky is old and wet
          with the sober reincarnations of mist soft
          and serene grey as e-waste burning overseas

or choose instead the mind as a diaspora of wind
ripping past obese, inflatable lawn ornaments
and as ebullient as the soul
of an asp worn
by Cleopatra.

          The days…these days
spend years in between themselves. In
between everything   sleepening. No matter.

And where is it exactly that you feel as safe as you can? And what
are the thoughts you can't abide, the ones whose words we'll never
hear
coming?

Listen and what you'll hear is

God gives you one gift: you get to be born, the choreographer Twyla
Tharp said. Thereafter
you've got to take care
of it yourself. Always see
the bigger picture. But you didn't, did
you? You spent
your days of grace in the operatic woods designing memes in
mirrors
merely memes that succeed simply
in making static in making nearby people look intensely
older. Poetry changing
nothing but it can eavesdrop:

and offer the protective language of care. Uh huh. A limping of
choreographies. Because time is losing its privacy, and I don't think
you should come round here
anymore.

Solastalgia

Thick strokes of orange-red, a few tossed down
in front of the eye, as if sliced from a red pepper,

and then a small pile of them, a drift of loose
logs ascending toward a rimmed colour I'd

never seen the sun advance before. A drum
burning though an oil haze. Several blurred

masts, chimneys, some sleeping industrial
cranes, one a forefinger of kingfisher blue-

grey, the colour steadying irresistible waves
undulating like missed opportunities

inside the viewer and two people in a boat,
their immediate reflection summoning the day

half opening, and threatening to disappear,
these waves, their reflections
                              that are bent
on impugning nothing.

*

I had none of these thoughts the first time I saw Monet's *Impression,*
Sunrise. I'd woken that morning in a sleeping bag on the ground at a
mountain campsite near Denver, Colorado. I was seventeen, my family
and some friends were asleep in the nearby motorhome, and there
were some birds I'd never seen before in the bushes: slate-coloured
juncos. Later on that trip from southern Ontario to California, I'd sleep
on top of the RV while in the desert because I wanted to stay in the
open but was afraid that a rattlesnake might come along during the
night.

   Monet's painting was on loan in the Denver art gallery. I had no idea
who he was. All I can remember from the afternoon I went there — by
myself, the first time I'd ever gone to such a place — was the Monet

and a room full of Chinese landscape paintings. Back then I'd planned on going to Kyoto to study Zen after completing high school, which meant that the scroll paintings immediately entered my ill-defined sense of interiority, providing an intimation of safety that was utterly different from the turbulence of adolescence. They also initiated a hazy yearning for a time in the future when I might gain whatever serenity those paintings held with their huge peaks, precisely shaped fir trees, and small human figures lucky enough to live undisturbed by the chaos that is usual among people. Moreover, these paintings made me understand that I needed to craft my life in such a way that I'd spend most of it living in the mountains.

Monet's painting offered something different. Until then, I hadn't realized that a human being could create colours that beautiful; until then, beauty like that was something that had come only from the natural world.

*

It's raining. I've been trying to recall more of that day, which began by my unzipping the worn sleeping bag, putting on cold clothes, when I woke a small distance from the pit of ashes from the campfire we'd had the previous night. But there's almost nothing in my memory. Except now, with today's rain, something comes back: I'd entered the art museum by chance: a thunderstorm had blown in from the mountains, and I'd taken shelter in the gallery. What has never gone away is that, wandering from room to room among paintings, I realized that, for the first time in my life, I actually knew where I was.

*

A chess piece meant to represent Napoleon, some mirtazapine, also a lion from a thrift store, the paint on his mane chipped, a copy of Lao Tzu's Tao Te Ching I bought for under two dollars and had with me when I was in Denver — these are some of the objects nearby. A small print of Impression, Sunrise, cut from a biography of the artist and placed inside a cheap wooden frame.

*

Unlike the lion (made in China, the date strangely on its belly — 1987) paused beneath the zebra-striped lamp I bought for a studio apartment after leaving my first marriage almost twenty years ago, the framed Monet is recent. I hadn't thought of this image for decades until this past summer when, allowing myself a single glass of red wine one evening, I looked at a sun that was the colour of the one in the painting, a fat luminescence utterly unknown to me in real life as a teenager because I'd never seen the sun leaning through smoke. But this was during this year's forest fire season in western Canada, and my lungs were sore because I've been an idiot and had smoked cigarettes for almost thirty years (taken up shortly after the day in Colorado). Gazing

> The valley spirit is not dead:
> They say it is the mystic female.
> Her gateway is, they further say,
> The base of earth and heaven.
>
> Constantly, and so forever.
> Use her without labour.
> *Lao Tzu, The Way of Life*

into Madge Lake near the Saskatchewan-Manitoba border, I played with my Polaroid camera. One hundred forty-nine years separate Monet's *Impression, Sunrise* from the photograph below, made possible because of wildfires zigzagging across three provinces. And only now do I recognize that the haze Monet painted in Le Havre was made by air pollution. And that our Winnebago, one of several luxurious RVs my father purchased during his traveling years, was indicative of a life that contributed to the destruction all around us.[1]

*

This destruction, the so-called Great Acceleration, taking off after World War II, was implicitly present while we innocently traveled with our two English friends across the United States. Bill, a retired geography teacher, who fought in the British army during this war, had been one of the troops that liberated Bergen-Belsen. Upon his retirement, he and his wife Kay had devoted themselves to a British charity called War on Want, traveling once to a village in Peru that they'd supported. The week before they arrived, however, the

---

1   Only a decade ago, Dad bemoaned spending $500 on gas travelling from visiting my family in Regina to Calgary in his final behemoth RV on a particularly windy trip. Such transcontinental journeys are over for him. Today we spoke, he hospitalized in a rehab centre in Ontario, and then most likely a long-term care facility. He'll never live independently again because he's become too fragile. Too damn old, as he puts it.

Sendero Luminoso (Shining Path) had destroyed the small boats the charity had purchased for the villagers. They're both gone now, Kay dying not long after turning one hundred in 2015 and Bill earlier. Two facts: during that trip they both were in constant movement in the RV, getting up from a seat near one window to take up a position near another. Why not just settle down for a game of chess? I suggested as we made our way through Nebraska. Because we'll never be through here again. World travelers, even standing out in the open, jostled between third-class train cars in Ecuador so they could see the jungle better, they never set foot in Germany. After Bergen-Belsen, Bill never wanted to see Germans of his own age and have to wonder what they'd known or done.

*

It's stopped raining and twenty-first-century geese are just now triangulating the sky with our deranged and ragged earth —

There's also been the flash of a pileated woodpecker, a male, its steady and garish passage up this tree and then the next one, one of its thoughts naked as a cliff, the others quickening to thickets of sap, insects, and ancestral memory —

*

On a trip from Saskatchewan to Ontario only a few years ago, my partner, Amy, our son Jakob, and I rented a cottage along the Bruce Peninsula. Snorkeled above a shipwreck, watched bats, and discovered that the word Tobermory contains dozens of other words, like a sac of spider eggs. Yet. Almost Bye-Bot. And we learned that we needed to book online a four-hour parking spot far in advance of when we planned to hike near Cyprus Lake. There's a paved pathway there now, instead of the narrow path twisting north over tree roots and sharply slanted, glaciated terrain.

No. Not for me. I don't want to see what that trail has become.

Solastalgia is grieving a lost landscape.

But our sense of what constitutes normality in the natural world is caged along with our day-to-day lives, lives trapped inside what appears to the times in which we live. Let's imagine someone in their sixties when I was a teenager. Someone who enjoyed scaling the boulders along the shoreline south of Tobermory — a person who could take in more than a dozen mergansers in a small bay, compared to the two I saw — this person with heavy, simple binoculars, might have spurned the snowmobiles that became a fad, a rupture across the snow when I was young, one of my uncles then making his living selling and repairing those new toys. Canary yellow. Night black. At full tilt: ninety decibels. Yamaha, Ski-Doo, Kawasaki.

Let's turbocharge.

But the oil crisis of 1979 struck first, and now global warming has obliterated the world that made sense to my uncle back then, a man who hunted moose when he got away from his shop. His face scored with chicken pox scars, his grandfather an immigrant from a village somewhere near Russia. His mind now corroded with Alzheimer's.

*

I never got to Japan, because a year after being in Colorado the usual happened. A woman arrived from out of nowhere; we moved in together; we headed toward university; we broke up; the cold blaze of addictions flared; more decades. On a window shelf near the lion there's a Tibetan singing bowl, and a gathering of stones lifted from glacial streams. Most days I choose one of them, cradle it in my hands, and then sit to observe my breathing, very often the most intellectually demanding thing I do that day, because my life has made me return to meditation. Buddhism, Pema Chödrön offers, is for people who don't have much time to waste.

*

But what's hardest and most necessary to hold, what diminishes everything, is the family of red-necked grebes I witnessed at Madge Lake this past summer, two adults and their three offspring, hidden for most of the day from the dirty heat, the air itchy with particulate, when they should have been out on the water feeding and taking delight in their home amidst reeds and decaying trees, and how they can never grasp what's been done to them.

Better order soon, the sky recommends, restaurant's closing.

*

Surveying my late middle age, watching its impossible and thinning accretions, I see lovely but inevitably battered marriages, the unexpected encounter of meeting one's own children, and today, especially within the October rain, I recall those scroll paintings, their background wash somewhere between ginger root, urine, and patient brass, and all along, I concentrate on breathing, take in the necessary time I once had to spend in the psych ward downtown; and I hold onto interior-exterior mountains, but they keep shifting, as they tend to do, having been given a quiet shove from behind by an ancient Buddhist sonnet composed from dead electricity, its actual shadow —

Yet each day releases
its precursors, depletions, and the vast migratory scrawl
of stilled cisterns   a phantasmagoria both strange
and exorbitant

the astonished human squall —

Nachträglichkeit↔Nachträglichkeit

Nothing is required of you, yet all must render an accounting.
— John Ashbery, *Flow Chart*

10:10

After thirty-six years, each of their faces has remained a clock showing 10:10, these drinkers in *The Beanery*, a large Edward Kienholz installation found in Amsterdam's Stedelijk Museum. I'm decades older than I was when I first peered into Kienholz's narrowly crowded bar, rampant with myriad affectionately collected objects and various life-size figures engaged in the blur of private conversation.

When I first encountered Kienholz, I was travelling with a backpack, sleeping in hostels and on the occasional park bench. I avoided the nearby Rijksmuseum as a matter of principle — the Old Masters were for people travelling by tourist buses, I thought, whereas I wanted art that spoke expressly to me in and of my own time — and so the Stedelijk became the first museum of modern art I'd ever visited.

(It took me decades to learn how wrong I was about the Old Masters.)

Nowadays, you stand in a line to go inside the Kienholz installation, but in 1978, you only had to lean over a divider and try to see as much as you could. Kienholz somehow condensed something in this piece that was different from anything I'd ever known or could even conceive of knowing. Life shifted for me just then, because nothing before had so vividly made me recognize the paucity of my experience. How could anything be like this? I recall sudden and new sensations: how narrowly I'd imagined things; the impossibility of the normal; the inherent, gaudy joy of excess.

Going through the other galleries (filled mostly with classical modernism, not that I knew the idea then), I saw unmistakable evidence that some people were capable of rejecting the tiresome orthodoxy upon which my background in southern Ontario had insisted. Kienholz & Co. promised it was possible to liberate oneself from conformity. Except that I've just made a Freudian slip because I didn't type "liberate" just now; I wrote that Kienholz promised it was possible to *live*. The distinction is important because it's one thing to desire emancipation from the restrictions a culture can inflict upon the spirit, but it is quite different to sense that there's something at stake that goes beyond rebellion. How can you learn to calibrate your life in such a way that you'll somehow succeed in justifying yourself to yourself? To say I had no idea is to simplify the yearning I assume most people feel when they are confronted with their inadequacies.

I returned to Kienholz in 2014 because what he'd made was decisive to me in ways it took years to understand, and I wanted to learn what, if anything, that early self would have to say to someone who had lived his entire lifetime twice over again, something as unimaginable then as it is now. I wanted to place myself in the exact location where an ambitious young man had determined to create a certain kind of future, and I wanted to peer at those clock-faced people once again to see what I might establish about the way time passes and whether I could find enough of that previous self to ascertain his judgment of what *he* had become.

I could have asked for directions, in the thoroughly renovated Stedelijk, to *The Beanery*'s new location, but I wanted to happen upon it by chance, just as I'd done the first time. After slowly going through a Jeff Wall exhibit, I saw what had to be the Kienholz from behind. I got in line and there was the (forgotten) August 28, 1964, newspaper in its box with its headlines "Children Kill Children in Viet Nam Riots" and "Photos Confirm Moon Volcano." Able to go inside this time, I noticed what I couldn't have observed before: the pay phone says, "out of order," and an ornately coiffed toy poodle has a place of its own on a bar stool next to its owner, a woman wearing a sullen wool shawl. Listening to the sounds coming from within the bar, wanting to rest my hand on the jukebox, I understood that Kienholz's miniature world holds a subdued violence, a sadness I hadn't detected when I'd stood outside the installation almost four decades before. The drinkers had now been there for a very long time, and it seemed that they were at the point of becoming broken upon solipsism, its battered repetitions, each one struck from a new anguish, and (always keeping an eye for something slightly unusual to happen or to find a new life in the next drink) there they were, there they stayed, each of them contained within a hermetic and slightly amber bubble of excess that will only pop when art like Kienholz's doesn't matter anymore or the installation's physical materials actually fall apart.[2]

2   After going through the line three times on one visit and twice on another, unfortunately, I uncovered neither a shred nor a whiff of a Proustian madeleine that might prompt the younger self either to eviscerate his elder or say: "Given our several failings, that'll do." There wasn't a single molecule of memory to be reclaimed. Though

After gaining some experience with marriage, divorce, and remarriage, wandering with confusion and tenderness amidst the multiple lives our children give us, writing too rarely, dealing with changes in health, and having pretty much understood why Kienholz has everyone in the bar, except the owner, with an unmoving clock as a face, I know that failure's close, but not really the right word for what's possible in a life, and there's nothing I can do to cut through the necessary accrual of events that both clog and dissipate the decades between my two selves.

Leaving the Stedelijk possibly for the last time — there's a particular grief a North American feels upon having to say goodbye to these impossibly distant galleries — I stood beneath its overhanging roof while an enormous downpour swept across Amsterdam's Museumplein. It seemed that all of Europe was raining, and as I took in the open space in front of me, I realized that much of what's driven my life was directly in view. The Rijkmuseum was at the other end of the park, and far less than a soccer field away from where I waited out the rain was Gabriël Metsustraat 6, Etty Hillesum's home during part of the war. I could nearly see the edge of the brick building where she'd lived (though I'd not known anything of her when I'd crossed the Museumplein for the first time), and only the day before, Rembrandt's self-portrait as the Apostle Paul — with his raised eyes, glancing past those of us in the room, his gaze detached, weary, and incredulous, mindful of compassion and futility, equally — told me that I must begin readying myself for troubles about to come. I then walked through the rain to look at Etty's window once again and tried to imagine her tearing "around the Skating Club like a drunken fool and address[ing] a few stupid remarks to the moon," while she attempted to touch the twentieth century with her fingertips possibly on that very spot, though the Skating Club has long since been demolished. Before heading north to my hotel room, in an eighteenth-century row house facing a canal, I first listened to the sounds made from wind that formed part of the memorial to the women and children sent to Ravensbrück, and then walked through the puddles on the basketball

---

I did chat with a museum guard who was there on my second visit, and she told me that she, too, loved the Kienholz because her mother, whom she guessed was about my age, had often taken her to see it when she was a child.

court near the Rijkmuseum, a recent addition to the square that might have perplexed Rembrandt.

If my younger, virginal self couldn't have imagined having a son who adores playing basketball, the middle-aged man finds it bizarre that almost everything that has mattered to my life was within view back then in 1978. It's so rare for time to be seeded within such a small space — within such an uncanny nearness — though *uncanny* isn't the right word to use. I consider Kienholz to have been the catalyst that created the sensibility that's closest to hand, but when I go through a box of old diaries, searching for the one I'd taken with me during that trip, I'm taken aback to find that Kienholz (and a visit to Dachau) isn't mentioned, not a single word.

On my last full day in Amsterdam in 2014, a Sunday, I went to a flea market and decided not to buy an antique postcard that showed a small group of Hitler Youth marching into a town's medieval square, one of them beating the drum around his neck and another holding aloft a banner with a swastika and tassels; on the reverse side of the card was a used Hitler stamp and a few German words I couldn't understand. Something makes me wish it was here as I write this sentence. Where was this card when I first saw the Kienholz? Who owned it then, and how did it get there from the 1930s? And just now, this moment it's

snowing amidst first light   and Amsterdam is impossibly far from
        here —

Saeculum: A Mixtape

The usual sense that your life is imprecisely
happening to you —

2.
No public obligation. Vespers creating nightmares
in OBJECTS — observe the face of a shower head
hyperventilating — and the endless sadness
of Thought TV, especially

3.
in the morning. COVID as the greatest
                                    muralist to come along
since global warming snuck into
our complacency with a can of flood
paint, *Monumento hysterico*, fire jamboree, and lemony
mosquito spill.
Meh.
Let's go get a grab bag
of inspirational Zombie
Formalism, let's rendezvous with cast-off
aerial photography of analog

4.
stockyards. Hello, hereditary embryologists. Our job to
transform
our ancestors' condition of ivory pubic hair
discovered after death. Best
stay put.
        It's to be expected: this just doesn't seem like the right sunlight
for an autopsy in the Lost City of Single Trees Missing
Their Children.
            There's so much talk these days of extraterrestrial
signatures, the doctrine of strangers, and, boiling it down, the glutton's

5.
nonplussed question   How come

A Year to Experiment

The question's a good one, but how about we move

on to the next sentence? Burning your excrement
can cause a forest fire. That amazing light bulb

decade: learning asperity, learning that the actuarial
odds are, you know, like *bad*-bad. This morning's
devoted to first ending, then studying, one of those

hurts-so-good kind of days. Join me. Make a plan
to keep yourself around, looking at the exit signs.
The mystery object on the lawn. In the mirror. People's
faces = a recovery of microseasons. Keeping vigil

beside the sleeping whatchamacallit in the corner. The things
I've done I'm not proud of — they keep spattering the floor.
Can't tell who's talking behind these grungy vines crying
out in unattainable joy. It's time to differentiate. Say. Can anyone
tell which of us is becoming unstuck, as another day shows

up, and then another? That life, the illicit one people swore

mixes disaster-grade CSI with *hiraeth*, a Welsh word expressing a deep longing for
   something that is gone,

      was as luscious to the fingertips as a canyon
      fluttering with sport jackets, each so, every one so
      defiant and so alive in its unspoiled dry-cleaning bag. A tranquility
      of nearby ghost refrigerators suddenly teeming —

What's Left Behind

After Painting Number 2 *by Franz Kline*

A bird bath filled with winter.

A seacoast crowding the sturdy escalator in the mall.

Looking for what's always there.

Finding what's backing away into the space opened by the newly
    dead: they're taking our
pictures, not with a counterfeit flash but from the busy darkness of
    their appearing, their
measuring, the way they're held to what's never part of the same.

Then living one thing only, it doesn't matter what it is?

As if what's here is abruptly remaining.

Suspended together, this littoral zone, when daylight leans across
    what you must eventually be.
Open & tireless, an
            arrival as borderless as naked as sight:
                the present disturbing its own alibi —

2.
Abiding and bygone, light waits
      nearby, this unhurried light
      its glacial air loosening
    what's dormant, what's
here
    for now:
        the faint
mercy
     of an eyelid, of the crooked
   fire in the pond

of the mind, the mercy of

where
we look next —

_____

And only a day later   the future's

trompe l'oeil coming straight
                        at you, stammering
with neglect

Notes

This book has been written over many years. The epigraph by Giorgio Agamben was chosen before COVID. If I've learned a great deal from Agamben about the nature of contemporaneity and the ethical problems of responding to Auschwitz, I don't share his critique (and rejection) of government regulations in the COVID pandemic.

Regarding punctuation: on occasion I use three periods…in such a manner. This punctuation indicates a pause, a delay, rather than ellipsis. When using ellipsis in a cited text, I use […]. Also, when referring to two European cities, Warsaw and Prague, I sometimes use the non-English spelling that would be familiar to either city's inhabitants.

Etty Hillesum's diaries form the invisible backdrop of this collection. Exuberant, yet aware of the monstrous confusions of her time, she was one of the Holocaust's most important diarists. Although her journals and letters extend only from 1941 to 1943, she managed in this work to embody the perplexities facing a young, ambitious writer who gradually came to understand that, as a Jewish woman living under Nazi-controlled Holland, she was unlikely to survive the war. Astutely perceptive of the psychologies of both victims and perpetrators, owing perhaps to her own depressive mood disorders, she wrote from within the chaos imposed by the Nazis, refused to go in hiding, and eventually perished at Auschwitz.

Other books that were important to my research are: Ulrich Baer, *Spectral Evidence: The Photography of Trauma*; Danuta Czech, *Auschwitz Chronicle, 1939–1945*; Debórah Dwork and Robert Jan van Pelt, *Auschwitz: 1270 to the Present*; Leon Greenman, *An Englishman in Auschwitz*; *Commandant of Auschwitz: The Autobiography of Rudolf Höss*; David Koker, *At the Edge of the Abyss: A Concentration Camp Diary, 1943–1944*; Primo Levi, *Survival in Auschwitz* and *The Voice of Memory: Interviews, 1961–1987*; Philip Mechanicus, *Year of Fear: A Jewish Prisoner Waits for Auschwitz*; Rainer Maria Rilke, *Duino Elegies* and *The Notebooks of Malte Laurids Brigge*.

*

"You can tell" responds to *A Lady Writing* (ca. 1662–65) by Johannes Vermeer, National Gallery of Art, Washington DC.

"They've never smelled jet fuel" is for Steve Gronert Ellerhoff. *The Hunters in the Snow* (1565), by Pieter Bruegel the Elder, is in the Kunsthistorisches Museum, Vienna. The word "rizzened" is of my own invention: Bruegel's unusual green seems to call for a new word.

"When You Sat for Dix": The biographical information regarding Dr. Heinrich Stadelmann is taken from *Glitter and Doom: German Portraits from the 1920s*, Ed. Sabine Rewald. References to Zeppelins are from Tom D. Crouch, *Lighter than Air: An Illustrated History of Balloons and Airships*. The firebombing of Dresden on February 13, 1945, destroyed most of the city, but Stadelmann survived by seeking shelter in his basement. His library was destroyed. By strange coincidence, Victor Klemperer, who was supposed to report to the Gestapo for deportation (i.e., removal to a camp) on February 13 — the night of the bombing raid — was saved because in the chaos that ensued, he was able to escape Dresden as an ordinary refugee, not as a fleeing Jew.

"The Temptations of Saint Anthony": The notion of "moral necrophilia" is taken from Luc Tuymans, in conversation with Adrian Locke, "The Art of Painting Nothing," in *James Ensor* (Royal Academy of Arts, 2016).

"The sky underlit with concrete": The artist who used a parachute for lighting in his studio was Mark Rothko.

"Everything After Follows from That" is fictional. While Grant Stonehouse and Len Carey are imagined, Dave Reynolds was a friend of the author; he shouldn't be confused with the historian of the same name.

"Yes, words really do": That words dream is an observation from Gaston Bachelard's *The Poetics of Reverie: Childhood, Language, and the Cosmos*. Yevgeny Khaldei was the Soviet photographer who took the famous picture of a soldier raising the Soviet flag over the Reichstag in 1945. That the photograph was staged and then manipulated is widely known; however, his work is much more than propaganda. Berlin's Martin-Gropius-Bau devoted an exhibition to his career in 2008.

"Second Worlds": Walker Evans's credo is taken from Philip Gefter, "Paul Graham and Seizing the Everyday Moments," *New York Times*, February 21, 2016, Arts and Design.

"Greenman's wife Else & his son Barney were wearing": Walter Benjamin provides an analysis of Klee's *Angelus Novus* in Thesis IX (from "Theses on the Philosophy of History") in *Illuminations*. The note about Wilfred von Oven comes from Laurence Rees, *Auschwitz: A New History*.

"The American pelicans are going to disappear": For information pertaining to the *Graf Zeppelin*, see Douglas Botting, *Dr. Eckener's Dream Machine: The Historic Saga of the Round-the-World Zeppelin*. The poet who helped me understand Bergman is Don Coles; see his book *A Dropped Glove in Regent Street* and interview in the *Wascana Review* (2006). See also Michael Herr, *Dispatches*; and *Etty: The Letters and Diaries of Etty Hillesum, 1941–1943*. The sentence "How one remembers certain things is beyond me" is from David Markson's *Wittgenstein's Mistress*.

"Disneyland"
Section 1: "This is the real Disneyland" is taken from the article "For Jihad Recruits, a Pipeline from Minnesota to Militancy" by Jack Healy, *New York Times*, September, 2014.
Section 2: The postcard of "Tank Man" is a drawing by Polyp, courtesy of *Ethical Consumer Magazine*; reference to Dutch children pretending to be Nazi paratroopers is from Miep Gies and Alison Leslie Gold, *Anne Frank Remembered: The Story of the Woman Who Helped to Hide the Frank Family*.
Section 4: Reference to the Field Museum is taken from a postcard, no attribution; reference to Vermeer is *The Art of Painting* (1666/68), Kunsthistorisches Museum, Vienna; reference to the forest King Jagiełło saved for hunting, HG, and European woodpeckers is from Alan Weisman's *The World without Us*; reference to African women is taken from Nicholas Kristof, "Two Women, Opposite Fortunes," *New York Times*, March 21, 2015, Sunday Opinion.
Section 5: Reference to cypress trees is from Walter Pater's *Marius the Epicurean*; reference to zombies etc. is taken from Dave Cullen's *Columbine*.
Section 6: In *Prague Pictures: Portraits of a City*, John Banville describes the practice of covering books with brown paper; reference to the immolated nun is from "Tibetan Nun Calling for End to China Rule and Dalai Lama's Return Sets Self on Fire," Edward Wong, *New York Times*, April 11, 2015. This section's final lines, "that day, he cautions me not to content myself / too quickly with my own definitions of the unknowable," are derived from Robert Antelme's observations in *The Human Race* that, when British soldiers liberated concentration camp inmates, they seemed to take in the prisoners' plights fairly quickly: "Most consciences are satisfied quickly enough, and need only a few words to reach a definite opinion of the unknowable."

"Two Letters": The reference to asparagus being an "Aryan" vegetable comes from Victor Klemperer, *I Will Bear Witness: A Diary of the Nazi Years, 1942–1945*; the Gargus Caves are described in *The Mind in the Cave: Consciousness and the Origins of Art*, by David Lewis-Williams. The admonition given to her children regarding refugees is from a note written to me by CG.

"Three young men, each holding a lobster": Hermann Langbein refers to Professor Günther Niethammer in *People in Auschwitz*.

"Always See the Bigger Picture": The Twyla Tharp quotation is from Gia Kourlas, "Twyla Tharp Wants You to Move," *New York Times*, October 24, 2019. The phrase "the protective language of care" is from Lauren Berlant, *Cruel Optimism*.

"Solastalgia" is a concept devised by Glenn A. Albrecht, who uses it to describe "the lived experience of distressing, negative environmental change." See his *Earth Emotions: New Words for a New World*.
   It wasn't until my early fifties that I was diagnosed with a learning disability. Until I learned of it much of my life was awry: simply inexplicable. And yet, despite my now having an awareness of the problem, anxiety continues to bloom like algae. The neuropsychologist who diagnosed me with NLD (nonverbal learning disability, though now it's called NVLD) explained the condition as "a developmentally based disorder that is often associated with deficits in nonverbal communication and perception." People with NVLD find technology intimidating, experience acute anxiety, inexplicable mood shifts, and find it hard to "adjust" to social difficulties. Given to obsession, we also consider our immediate environments to be intrinsically threatening. Apparently, we usually retreat into solitude, and are susceptible to depression. (The news that my chronic depression was likely the result of the learning disability was astonishing.) People with NVLD are also prone to substance abuse. Apparently, I've had this condition for all of my life, and have "historically compensated" for these weaknesses by relying on verbal skills and developing a keen memory. Learning to use words became a form of psychic survival. The condition has also resulted in manageable OCD. In 2020 I was hospitalized owing to complications from this disorder.

"10:10": The notion that rain was sweeping all across Europe alludes to Max Richter's composition "Europe, After the Rain," from the album *Memoryhouse*.
   The photograph showing the canal was taken on the north side of Nieuwe Keizersgracht, just west of where the Jewish Council had its office. The plaques on the cement identify Jewish people, mostly families, who lived there before being deported. Their ages are recorded, along with the dates and locations of their deaths.

"Saeculum: A Mixtape": The concept *saeculum* was first used by the Etruscans. Originally it meant the time from the moment that something happened (for example the founding of a city) until the point in time that all people who had lived at the first moment had died. At that point a new saeculum would start. (s.v. "saeculum," Oxford Classical Dictionary)

"A Year to Experiment": Describing the various human activities that inadvertently result in forest fires, Clare Frank mentions "campers who decided to burn their excrement." See Dhruv Khullar, "Hazy Days," Talk of the Town, *New Yorker*, July 3, 2023. For the quotation "which mixes disaster-grade CSI with *hiraeth*, a Welsh word expressing a deep longing for something that is gone" see Sam Knight, "Chaos Theory," Letter from the UK, *New Yorker*, May 22, 2023.

Acknowledgements

Because it took almost two decades to write this book, many people offered help, sometimes by reading and commenting on pieces, making reading suggestions, and sharing time for discussion. Without the ongoing support of my partner, the ceramicist and conceptual artist Amy Snider, and my children, Andy, Jesse, and Jakob, I wouldn't have been able to complete the book. These poems and essays are dedicated to them. And I further dedicate the book to birds everywhere.

I would like to thank Don Coles, Don McKay (who facilitated a Sage Hill Writing Retreat in 2015), Barry Dempster, and Colin Smith for their invaluable advice on the manuscript.

Many friends over the years have been generous to read drafts of various pieces in the book. Let me especially thank Philip Charrier, a colleague and friend who has always offered support. A single conversation with him substantially altered the way I write. Susan Lohafer, likely the most gifted reader I know, has blessed me with a delightful and intricate conversation about literature, ethics, and the world that goes back for decades. I treasure the long talks I've had with Ben Salloum; his erudition, wisdom, and wide-ranging intelligence have helped me understand my subject matter more deeply. Jeremy Desjarlais has helped me understand my poetry in new ways. Also, thanks to the members of the poetry workshop group POV (Jes Battis, Troni Grande, Tracy Hamon, Medrie Purdham, Melanie Schnell, Tara Dawn Solheim, and Kathleen Wall), who helped make the poems cleaner. Some others — Derek Brown, Jason Demers, Paul Endo, gillian harding-russell, Craig Melhoff, kat Nogue, Jeremy Stewart, Dan Tysdal, and Ken Wilson — have offered their wisdom when times became hard.

Decades of teaching at the University of Regina have allowed me to interact with many wonderful students, too numerous to name individually. I would, though, like to offer thanks to Joel Blechinger, Jesse Desjarlais, and Sarah Fahie for their thoughtful, indeed sparkling emails and helpful reading recommendations. The English department's willingness to allow instructors to develop their own idiosyncratic courses has enabled me to combine teaching with research and writing.

I also wish to thank Jim Johnstone for his steady, generous support and excellent guidance. When times became very difficult, his belief in my writing was (and remains) rejuvenating. Finally, thank you to copy editor Martin Ainsley, proofreader Sarah Ratchford, and Alan Sheppard and Julie Scriver at Goose Lane Editions for their painstaking care with the manuscript.

Some of the material in this collection has appeared in different forms in the following journals and presses: the Alfred Gustav Press, *Angry Old Man*, the *Antigonish Review*, *Fiddlehead*, *Grain*, the *Puritan*, and *Vallum*. My thanks to the editors for publishing my work.

Michael Trussler's work engages with the beauty and violence of the twentieth and twenty-first centuries from a neurodivergent, fluid perspective. His writing encompasses several genres and modes of expression, ranging from the lyrical to the avant-garde. Trussler teaches English at the University of Regina and is the author of seven books, including *10:10*; *The History Forest*, winner of the Saskatchewan Book Award for Poetry; the short fiction collection, *Encounters*, winner of the Saskatchewan Book of the Year Award; and a memoir entitled *The Sunday Book*, which won the Saskatchewan Book Award in both the Non-Fiction and City of Regina categories. Deeply compelled by the natural world, Trussler hikes in the Canadian Rockies at every opportunity.